EDGE
BOOKS™

FANTASY
FIELD GUIDES

A FIELD GUIDE TO

Dragons, Trolls,
and other Dangerous Monsters

BY A. J. SAUTTER

CAPSTONE PRESS
a capstone imprint

Edge Books are published by Capstone Press,
1710 Roe Crest Drive, North Mankato, Minnesota 56003
www.capstonepub.com

Library of Congress Cataloging-in-Publication Data
Sautter, Aaron.
A field guide to dragons, trolls, and other dangerous monsters / by A.J. Sautter.
pages cm.—(Edge books. Fantasy field guides)
Includes bibliographical references and index.
Summary: "Describes the features and characteristics of dangerous fantasy creatures
in a quick-reference format"—Provided by publisher.
ISBN 978-1-4914-0691-5 (library binding)
ISBN 978-1-4914-0695-3 (paperback)
ISBN 978-1-4914-0699-1 (eBook PDF)
1. Dragons—Juvenile literature. 2. Trolls—Juvenile literature.
3. Monsters—Juvenile literature. I. Title.
GR830.D7S278 2015
398.24'54—dc23   2014010191

Editorial Credits
Sarah Bennett, designer; Kelly Garvin, media researcher;
Katy LaVigne, production specialist

Photo Credits
Dreamstime/Chorazin3d, 23; Capstone Press: Colin Ashcroft, 1, 16, 20, Jonathan
Mayer, 13, Martin Bustamante, 18, 26, Tom McGrath, cover, 8, 14; Shutterstock:
dalmingo, 28, firstear, 25, Fotokostic, 4, 11, LongQuattro, 1, Melkor, 7

Artistic Credits
Shutterstock: argus, foxie, homydesign, Kompaniets Taras, Lora liu, Oleg Golovnev,
Picsfire, Rashevska Nataliia, xpixel

Printed in the United States of America in Stevens Point, Wisconsin.
052014   008092WZF14

Table of Contents

A World of Dangerous Monsters

The world is a dangerous place. It's overflowing with deadly monsters waiting for a chance to attack—and possibly eat—human beings. Giants, trolls, and ogres like to **ambush** and rob unwitting travelers in the mountains. And dragons enjoy attacking cities and villages to add to their treasure **hoards**. At least, tales and legends around the world would like us to believe these fantastic monsters and others are real.

But the truth is that dragons, trolls, and other dangerous monsters live only in people's imaginations. People have been telling stories about them for hundreds of years. Today these awe-inspiring monsters are more popular than ever. They show up in everything from books and movies to roleplaying games, video games, TV shows, and more. Why do these monsters keep showing up in our stories? Perhaps it's because we wish they were real. They offer us a sense of excitement and adventure that is rarely found in most people's everyday lives.

Let's imagine for a while that dangerous fantasy monsters are real and alive in the world today. If you went looking for them, would you know what to look for? Where do these creatures live? What do they eat? How do they behave? Get ready for a wild adventure as we look at some fantastic monsters and how they would live if they were real.

ambush ⇢ to make a surprise attack

hoard ⇢ a large collection of something, usually treasure

Red Dragons

Size:
150 feet (46 meters)
long or more;
wingspans up to
180 feet (55 m)

Habitat:
lairs are usually
found in deep caves
in the mountains

Diet:
deer, sheep, cattle,
pigs, and other
small animals; prefer
humans when possible

Life Cycle: Female red dragons lay two or three eggs about every 150 years. To keep the eggs hot, females breathe fire on them twice a day until they hatch. The **wyrmlings** are then left to care for themselves. Red dragons reach adulthood at about 200 years. They can live to more than 2,500 years old.

Physical Features: Red dragons are a bright shade of red when they hatch. As they age their scales become a dark red or red-gold color. Red dragons have razor-sharp claws and teeth. They also have powerful whiplike tails used to bash enemies to the ground. Of course, red dragons are most famous for their flaming breath weapon. When threatened or angered, they create a fiery blast hot enough to melt steel.

Behavior: Red dragons are incredibly prideful and greedy. They also have fierce tempers. They'll attack and kill anyone who insults them or intrudes on their territory. Red dragons guard their huge treasure hoards jealously. If even a single coin is stolen, red dragons will fly into a terrible rage. They'll destroy nearby farms and villages to find and punish the thieves.

★★★ FANTASY ALL-STAR

Red dragons love to be praised and admired. In the book *The Hobbit* by J.R.R. Tolkien, Bilbo Baggins meets the huge dragon Smaug. Bilbo uses several compliments to distract Smaug before escaping with a golden cup.

lair ⋯ a place where a wild animal lives and sleeps

wyrmling ⋯ a baby dragon

7

White Dragons

Size:
about 100 feet
(31 m) long;
wingspans up to
120 feet (37 m)

Habitat:
icy caves on mountain
peaks, polar areas,
or large icebergs

Diet:
fish, seals, caribou,
and sometimes whales

Life Cycle: Females lay five to six eggs about every 100 years. They bury the eggs in ice or snow to keep them cold. The wyrmlings care for themselves after hatching. White dragons become adults at about age 100 and can live up to 2,000 years.

Physical Features: Young white dragons are very light in color. As they age their scales darken slightly and sometimes turn light blue. Most dragons have horns on their heads. But white dragons instead have a bony **frill** to help protect their necks. Like other dragons, white dragons have wickedly sharp claws and teeth and a strong whiplike tail. When cornered they rely on their icy breath weapon. Their icy cold blast can freeze enemies solid in an instant.

Behavior: White dragons spend a great deal of time hunting for prey. However, they rarely eat anything without letting it freeze solid first. They may use their breath weapon to freeze their food, but they usually allow it to freeze normally outside. White dragons aren't as ferocious as red dragons or as cruel as black dragons. But they do have long memories. They are known to seek revenge for insults that took place many years before. Like most dragons, white dragons love treasure. But they especially enjoy glittering diamonds and silver coins.

frill -- a bony collar that fans out around an animal's neck

Black Dragons

Size:
up to 120 feet
(37 meters) long;
wingspans up to
150 feet (46 m)

Habitat:
bogs, swamps, or dark
jungles; lairs are often
in caves with hidden
underwater entrances

Diet:
fish, birds, turtles,
alligators, deer,
opossums, muskrats

Life Cycle: Female black dragons hide one or two eggs under rotting plants about every 120 years. Their young are left to hatch on their own and take care of themselves. Black dragons become adults at about 150 years and live up to 2,200 years.

Physical Features: Also known as swamp dragons, black dragons have thin, bony bodies. As they age their black scales turn lighter until they look dark purple. The skin of most black dragons is thin and appears diseased. Their wings tend to tear easily, so most don't fly well. Like most dragons, black dragons have deadly claws, teeth, and tails. Their powerful acid breath weapon can dissolve the thickest of armor.

Behavior: Black dragons are known for their cruel nature. They enjoy hunting and killing creatures simply to cause them pain. But black dragons can also be cowardly. They quickly retreat from more dangerous opponents. Black dragons love to hoard treasure. They tend to prefer gold coins over gems or other valuable items.

bog ‑ an area of wet, spongy land, often filled with dead and rotting plants

★ ★ ★

FANTASY ALL-STAR

One of the most powerful dragons ever
written about was Ancalagon the Black.
In *The Silmarillion* by J.R.R. Tolkien,
this dragon was so huge that his wings
blocked out the sun.

Eastern Dragons

Size:
more than 200 feet
(61 m) long

Habitat:
caves near rivers and
lakes with hidden
underwater entrances

Diet:
fish, birds, deer,
sheep, goats, rabbits,
squirrels, and other
small animals

Life Cycle: Eastern dragons are extremely rare. Females lay one pearl-like egg about every 500 to 1,000 years. It takes about 500 years for the egg to hatch. Young eastern dragons grow very slowly. It takes up to 2,000 years for these dragons to reach adulthood. Eastern dragons live especially long lives. They are thought to live for more than 8,000 years.

Physical Features: Eastern dragons are often brightly colored with red, yellow, blue, or green scales. Eastern dragons appear to be a combination of parts from other animals. Their heads are shaped like a camel's, and they have antlers like a deer's. Their bodies look like giant snakes with fish scales. And their feet are tipped with sharp talons like those of an eagle. Eastern dragons are not known to have a breath weapon. They don't have wings, but they do have a magical ability to fly.

Behavior: Eastern dragons can be deadly in a fight against their enemies. However, eastern dragons are known for being wise and helpful toward humans. They are often thought to be able to control the weather. During bad **droughts**, eastern dragons are sometimes said to bring rain to help farmers' crops grow. Eastern dragons are not greedy for treasure like other dragons. But they do enjoy collecting colorful gemstones such as rubies, emeralds, and opals.

drought -- a long period of weather with little or no rainfall

Mountain Giants

Size:
more than 45 feet
(13 m) tall

Habitat:
usually large caves
in the mountains;
some giants build
large homes in secret
hidden valleys

Diet:
deer, elk, caribou,
sheep, and goats;
occasionally humans

Life Cycle: Female mountain giants have one baby about every 40 years. Mothers care for their children much like humans do. However, giants live much longer and grow more slowly than humans. They are considered adults at about age 50 and usually live between 600 and 700 years.

Physical Features: Other than their huge size, mountain giants are very similar to humans. However, their skin is tough and is almost always a stonelike gray color. For this reason they are often called Stone Giants. They usually have black, brown, or fiery red hair. Most males also grow huge, bushy beards. Giants have no natural weapons other than their enormous strength.

Behavior: Mountain giants like to live alone and be left alone. They can become angry and dangerous when disturbed by outsiders. Their favorite weapon is often a huge spiked club, which they use to smash enemies to the ground. Giants are not normally eager to fight. But they do enjoy hurling huge boulders at each other in mock combats. After these mock battles, mountain valleys often look as if a large landslide has taken place with piles of rubble everywhere.

Fact Giants in stories and roleplaying games often have magical abilities. Fire giants create and fight with magical flaming weapons. Frost giants attack enemies with magical blasts of ice and snow. Storm giants can attack with howling winds and bolts of lightning.

Cyclopes

Size:
about 15 feet
(4.6 m) tall

Habitat:
mountain caves or
the ruins of old
castles and other
stone buildings

Diet:
sheep, goats,
deer, rabbits,
squirrels, and
other small
animals

Life Cycle: Female Cyclopes have one child every 30 to 50 years. They care for their children until they become adults at around age 100. Cyclopes usually live between 450 to 500 years.

Physical Features: Cyclopes are distantly related to giants and share some similar features. They have stocky bodies and large, strong hands. Their skin is tough and is often red-brown or stony gray in color. Most Cyclopes do not have any hair, but a few may have thin black or brown beards. The Cyclopes' most notable feature is the single large eye in the middle of their foreheads. It's thought that their eyes can cause crippling fear in those who look directly at them.

Behavior: Cyclopes usually live alone. They often spend their days protecting their lairs and raising herds of animals. Many Cyclopes are also clever **blacksmiths**. They are known for making high-quality weapons and armor. It's thought that Cyclopes also create powerful magical items in their secret **forges** deep inside volcanoes.

> **Fact** According to one Greek myth, several Cyclopes helped the god Hephaestus become a master blacksmith. They helped him create powerful magical weapons and armor for the gods. These included Zeus' lightning bolts, Poseidon's **trident**, and Apollo's bow.

blacksmith -- someone who makes and fixes things made of iron or steel

forge -- a special furnace in which metal is heated

trident -- a long spear with three sharp points at its end

Ettins

Size:
about 20 to 25 feet
(6 to 7.6 m) tall

Habitat:
dark underground
caves in remote
rocky locations

Diet:
deer, elk, sheep,
goats, rabbits, and
other small animals

Life Cycle: Female ettins have one child about every five years. Young ettins grow very quickly. They are able to care for themselves and leave home in about three years. Because ettins age so fast, they don't live as long as other giants do. Most ettins live only 90 to 100 years.

Physical Features: Like other giants, ettins have very tall, muscular bodies. These strange creatures also have two or more heads. Each head controls a different part of the body. Their thick skin is tough and protects them as a natural form of armor. Their hair is often long and stringy and is usually black or dark brown. Some ettins may also grow thick, bushy beards.

Behavior: Ettins are normally active at night and will eat any meat they can catch, including humans. Ettins never bathe and are usually covered in layers of smelly dirt and grime. They normally live alone in dark caves that stink of decaying food. Ettins do not like to be disturbed and will attack anyone who gets near their homes. In spite of their multiple heads, ettins aren't very intelligent. However, they are skilled at using multiple weapons in battle. Ettins are fierce fighters and will usually fight to the death. An ettin's favorite weapons are often a pair of spiked clubs.

Ogres

Size:
8 to 10 feet
(2.4 to 3 m) tall

Habitat:
dark, damp caves in foothills near mountains; some live near stinking bogs or swamplands

Diet:
almost any animal, including humans; they especially like snakes, snails, slugs, grubs, and other slimy creatures

Life Cycle: Female ogres have one or two babies nearly every year. Young ogres grow very quickly and reach adulthood by age 3. However, because of their violent nature and lifestyle, ogres rarely live more than 35 years. The oldest ogres tend to live only about 50 years.

Physical Features: Ogres share several features of both giants and trolls. Their bodies are muscular and they are amazingly strong. They have incredibly tough skin, which is often green or gray-green in color. Ogres also often have club hands, shortened legs, hunched backs, and other **deformities**. Some ogres have sharp tusks growing from their bottom jaws.

Behavior: Ogres are naturally very violent and cruel. They enjoy torturing enemies and love hearing them cry out in pain. Even in their own families, ogres enjoy playing cruel pranks that often result in injuries to others. Ogres aren't very intelligent and don't have useful skills other than fighting. For this reason, ogre tribes go on night **raids** to steal the food and goods they need from nearby villages. Although the sun doesn't harm them, ogres hate sunlight and avoid it if possible.

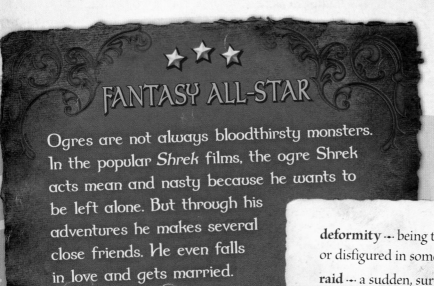

★ ★ ★

FANTASY ALL-STAR

Ogres are not always bloodthirsty monsters. In the popular *Shrek* films, the ogre Shrek acts mean and nasty because he wants to be left alone. But through his adventures he makes several close friends. He even falls in love and gets married.

deformity ⇢ being twisted, bent, or disfigured in some way

raid ⇢ a sudden, surprise attack on a place

Cave Trolls

Size:
10 to 12 feet
(3 to 3.7 m) tall

Habitat:
deep, dark caves
in hills and
mountain regions

Diet:
sheep, goats, deer,
horses, rabbits;
occasionally dwarves
or humans

Life Cycle: Female cave trolls give birth to one baby about every five years. Young trolls grow quickly. They are usually considered adults by age 10. Nobody knows how long cave trolls live, but it is thought they normally live between 65 and 75 years.

Physical Features: Cave trolls are distantly related to mountain giants, which helps explain their huge size and strength. Their arms are usually longer than their legs, which gives them an apelike **stance**. Cave trolls' tough skin strongly resembles stone in color. Cave trolls also have mouths filled with sharp jagged teeth and two large tusks.

Behavior: Cave trolls have one great weakness. If exposed to direct sunlight, their bodies turn to solid stone. For this reason, they sleep in their caves during the day and are active only at night. Cave trolls have huge appetites and spend most of their time looking for food. When they can't find enough food in the wild, they will steal animals from nearby farms. Some cave trolls live with groups of **orcs** in the mountains. In exchange for food, they will fight with the orcs to ambush unsuspecting travelers.

stance ⁓ the position of someone's arms, legs, and body

orc ⁓ a dangerous and ugly humanlike fantasy monster

Forest Trolls

Size:
12 to 15 feet
(3.7 to 4.6 m) tall

Habitat:
dark caves found in
thick forests in
northern regions

Diet:
any creature they
can catch, including
dwarves and humans

Life Cycle: Forest trolls live in remote locations and are rarely seen. For this reason, it is unknown how often they reproduce or how long they live. However, it is thought that forest trolls may live up to 200 years.

Physical Features: Forest trolls have huge, muscular bodies. Like cave trolls, they have long arms and short legs. They often stand hunched forward with their fists resting on the ground. Forest trolls have gray or green-gray skin, but their bodies are often covered in coarse brown hair. These trolls are recognizable for their huge mouths filled with jagged, rotten teeth. They also have large tusks jutting out from their lower jaws.

Behavior: Little is known about forest trolls. They always live alone and have rarely been seen. It's thought that they spend most of their time roaming the forest looking for food. Forest trolls do show some signs of intelligence. A few reports state that these creatures wear armor and carry weapons. They will fiercely attack intruders who wander into their territory. They are also said to be able to track enemies through the thickest forests.

Fact Trolls are popular creatures in many legends from Scandinavia. Stories often describe trolls as being big, slow, and dim-witted. In several stories, heroes easily trick trolls into harming themselves or allowing the heroes to escape.

Scandinavia ⋯ a region in northern Europe that includes the countries of Norway, Sweden, Finland, and Denmark

Swamp Trolls

Size:
8 to 10 feet
(2.4 to 3 m) tall

Habitat:
swamps and bogs in
tropical regions

Diet:
fish, crawfish, frogs,
snakes, muskrats,
alligators, humans

Life Cycle: Swamp trolls give birth to one child about every three years. The young grow quickly and reach adulthood by age 8. Swamp trolls are rarely seen, so it is unknown how long they live. Some people believe they live between 90 and 100 years.

Physical Features: Swamp trolls aren't as large as other trolls. But they do have muscular bodies and are incredibly strong. Their skin is usually dark green. But they are often covered in stinking mud, so their skin looks black. Swamp trolls have strong hands tipped with wicked claws used to slash at their prey.

Swamp trolls can quickly **regenerate**. They quickly heal from wounds that would kill other creatures. If a troll loses an arm or leg, the missing limb will regrow within five minutes. The only thing that can completely destroy a swamp troll is fire or acid.

Behavior: Swamp trolls are little more than savage beasts. They are not intelligent and can't speak. They spend most of their time hunting for their next meal. Although sunlight doesn't harm swamp trolls, their eyes are sensitive to it. They avoid leaving their lairs during the day and are active only at night. Swamp trolls are very aggressive and violent. They will attack humans and other creatures on sight.

regenerate -- to heal from an injury or regrow lost limbs

Legends Around the World

𝔚 Western Dragons

Stories about dangerous, fire-breathing dragons come mainly from Europe. These stories often feature brave heroes who fight and kill deadly dragons to save innocent people. Some of these stories include "Beowulf" from England, "Sigurd and Fafnir" from Scandinavia, and "Saint George and the Dragon" from Turkey.

𝔈 Eastern Dragons

In Asian stories dragons are often kind and helpful. In the story "The Four Dragons" from China, four helpful dragons bring rain to help farmers' crops. In one Japanese story, "Ryujin" is a dragon king who controls the ocean tides and the weather. And one Vietnamese myth describes how the dragon "Lac Long Quan" helped create the Vietnamese people.

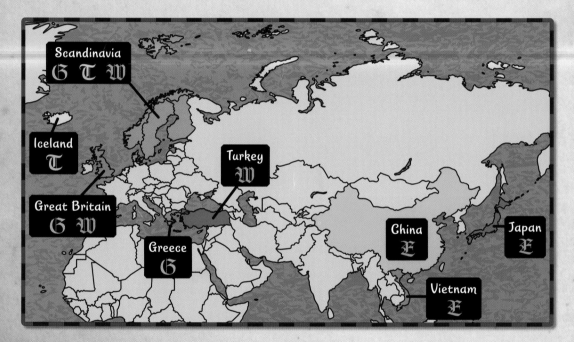

𝔊 Giants

Stories about giants come from around the world. In Scandinavia Norse myths are filled with frost giants, fire giants, and mountain giants. The story "Jack the Giant Killer" comes from England and features a hero who kills several nasty giants. Myths from ancient Greece are also filled with giant monsters such as the one-eyed Cyclops.

𝔗 Trolls

Several rock formations in Iceland and Scandinavia remind people of trolls that have turned to stone in the sunlight. These "stone trolls" have inspired several folktales in these countries. Stories such as "The Three Billy Goats Gruff" and "Peer Gynt" feature mean and nasty trolls that aren't very smart.

Test Your Knowledge

Think you know everything about dragons, trolls, and giants? Take this short quiz to test your knowledge. Do you have what it takes to become an expert on fantasy creatures?

1 If a cave troll catches you in the woods you should:

- **A.** try to convince him to let you go.
- **B.** fight your way past him.
- **C.** keep talking to him until the sun rises.

2 Ettins have more than one head and usually tend to:

- **A.** be more intelligent than other giant races.
- **B.** be very skilled with multiple weapons.
- **C.** argue with themselves a lot.

3 A white dragon's favorite kind of treasure is:

- **A.** sparkling diamonds and silver coins.
- **B.** colorful jewels and gems.
- **C.** golden cups and coins.

4 If you meet a red dragon you should:

- **A.** use compliments to distract it until you can escape.
- **B.** stare at its eyes.
- **C.** try to take as much of its treasure as possible.

5 If you're battling a swamp troll, the best weapon to use is:

- **A.** a magic sword.
- **B.** fire.
- **C.** magic spells and potions.

6 Ogres raid nearby farms and villages at night to:

- **A.** steal food and supplies they can't make themselves.
- **B.** avoid sunlight.
- **C.** both A and B.

Answers: 1:C, 2:B, 3:A, 4:A, 5:B, 6:C

Glossary

ambush (AM-bush) ⋯ to make a surprise attack

blacksmith (BLAK-smith) ⋯ someone who makes and fixes things made of iron or steel

bog (BAWG) ⋯ an area of wet, spongy land, often filled with dead and rotting plants

deformity (di-FORM-ih-tee) ⋯ being twisted, bent, or disfigured in some way

drought (DROUT) ⋯ a long period of weather with little or no rainfall

forge (FORJ) ⋯ a special furnace in which metal is heated

frill (FRIL) ⋯ a bony collar that fans out around an animal's neck

hoard (HORD) ⋯ a large collection of something, usually treasure

lair (LAYR) ⋯ a place where a wild animal lives and sleeps

orc (ORK) ⋯ a dangerous and ugly humanlike fantasy monster

raid (RAYD) ⋯ a sudden, surprise attack on a place

regenerate (re-JEN-uh-rayt) ⋯ to heal from an injury or regrow lost limbs

Scandinavia (skan-duh-NAYV-ee-uh) ⋯ a region in northern Europe that includes the countries of Norway, Sweden, Finland, and Denmark

stance (STANS) ⋯ the position of someone's arms, legs, and body

trident (TRY-dent) ⋯ a long spear with three sharp points at its end

wyrmling (WURM-ling) ⋯ a baby dragon

Read More

Caldwell, S.A. *Dragonworld: Secrets of the Dragon Domain*. Philadelphia: RP Kids, 2011.

Knudsen, Shannon. *Giants, Trolls, and Ogres*. Fantasy Chronicles. Minneapolis: Lerner Publications Co., 2010.

Malam, John. *Giants*. Mythologies. Irvine, Cal.: QEB Pub., 2009.

Internet Sites

FactHound offers a safe, fun way to find Internet sites related to this book. All of the sites on FactHound have been researched by our staff.

Here's all you do:

Visit *www.facthound.com*

Type in this code: 9781491406915

Check out projects, games and lots more at
www.capstonekids.com

Index